WILD WORK

WHO WALKS THE TIGHTROPE?
WORKING AT A CIRCUS

Mary Meinking

www.raintreepublishers.co.uk
Visit our website to find out more information about Raintree books.

To order:
☎ Phone 0845 6044371
🗎 Fax +44 (0) 1865 312263
🖳 Email myorders@raintreepublishers.co.uk

Customers from outside the UK please telephone +44 1865 312262

Raintree is an imprint of Capstone Global Library Limited, a company incorporated in England and Wales having its registered office at 7 Pilgrim Street, London, EC4V 6LB – Registered company number: 6695582

Edited by David Andrews, Nancy Dickmann, and Rebecca Rissman
Designed by Victoria Allen
Picture research by Liz Alexander
Leveled by Marla Conn, with Read-Ability.
Originated by Dot Gradations Ltd
Printed and bound in China by Leo Paper Products

ISBN 978 1 4062 1680 6 (hardback)
14 13 12 11 10
10 9 8 7 6 5 4 3 2 1

British Library Cataloguing in Publication Data
Meinking, Mary.
Who walks the tightrope? : working at a circus. -- (Wild work)
1. Circus--Juvenile literature. 2. Circus performers--Juvenile literature.
I. Title II. Series
791.3'023-dc22

Acknowledgements
The author and publisher are grateful to the following for permission to reproduce copyright material:

Alamy pp. 7 (© Ambient Images Inc), 12 (© Agripicture Images), 13 (© picturesbyrob), 17 (© tony French), 20 (© RubberBall), 24 (© ClassicStock), 29 (© Picture Contact); Corbis pp. 5 (© Steve Marcus), 10 (© John Lund), 15 (© Henry Diltz), 16 (© Tom Fox/Dallas Morning News), 18 (© Juan Medina/Reuters), 19 (© Aristide Economopoulos/Star Ledger); Getty Images pp 8 (Pascal Guyot/AFP), 9 (Zigy Kaluzny/Stone), 11 (Darren McCollester), 14 (Ian Shaw/Stone), 25 (Stan Honda/AFP), 26 (Monaco Centre de Presse-pool), 28 (Sandra Mu); Guinness World Records Smashed on Sky 1/Andi Southam p. 21; Photolibrary pp. 6 (White), 22 (L SA House - Willinger/Superstock), 23 (Motor-Presse Syndication/Superstock), 27 (Robert Ginn/Index Stock Imagery); Shutterstock p. 4 (© Losevsky Pavel).

Background design features reproduced with permission of Shutterstock (© hcreate).

Cover photograph reproduced with permission of TopFoto (©RIA Novosti).

Every effort has been made to contact copyright holders of material reproduced in this book. Any omissions will be rectified in subsequent printings if notice is given to the publisher.

Some words are shown in bold, **like this**. You can find out what they mean by looking in the glossary.

Contents

Under the big top

Step right up for a sneak peek at the circus! **Performers** fly through the air. Others tie themselves in knots. Many circuses move from town to town.

A modern type of circus is called a **cirque** (say *SURK*). People perform in these circuses. The performers' acts often tell a story.

Step right up!

The **ringmaster** keeps the show going.
He or she tells people which act is next.
Ringmasters talk about the danger
or special talent of each act.

Most **performers** don't speak during the show. The ringmaster speaks for them. Some ringmasters act along with the performers.

Walking on air

High in the air, tightrope walkers move along a wire. Many walkers carry a pole to help them keep their balance. Some do **somersaults** on the wire. Others juggle or do tricks as a group.

tightrope

DID YOU KNOW?

Tightrope walkers wear thin shoes so their feet can grab the wire.

Flying high

A pair of **trapeze** artists swings high above the crowd. One hangs by his knees. The other slides off her trapeze and does flips in the air. Her partner catches her.

trapeze

Other **aerialists** (say *AIR-ee-uh-lists*) perform on a fabric rope hanging from the ceiling. They climb, swing, and spin on the rope.

What daredevils!

Daredevils do dangerous things to amaze the crowds. Human **cannonballs** are shot out of cannons. There's no real explosion—a blast of air shoots them out. They land safely in a net or on a huge bag of air.

DID YOU KNOW?

Human cannonballs fly faster than some cars go!

Fire **performers** eat fire, breathe fire, or juggle things that are on fire. They know the secrets of doing fire tricks so they don't get burned. Sword swallowers shock crowds with their tricks.

You're not a circus performer. So don't try these tricks at home!

Tossed in the air

Circus jugglers throw almost anything. Most use balls, rings, or clubs. Some juggle flaming torches or chainsaws.

Because you're not a circus performer, you shouldn't try these dangerous tricks at home!

Jugglers start off with three things. Then more are added. Some jugglers work as a team passing things back and forth.

Tied in knots

Can you stretch your legs behind your head? Then you're born to be a **contortionist** (say *con-TORE-shun-ist*). These **performers** stretch a lot so they can bend into strange shapes.

Some contortionists can squeeze into a box the size of a microwave oven. Others can squeeze through an unstrung tennis racket.

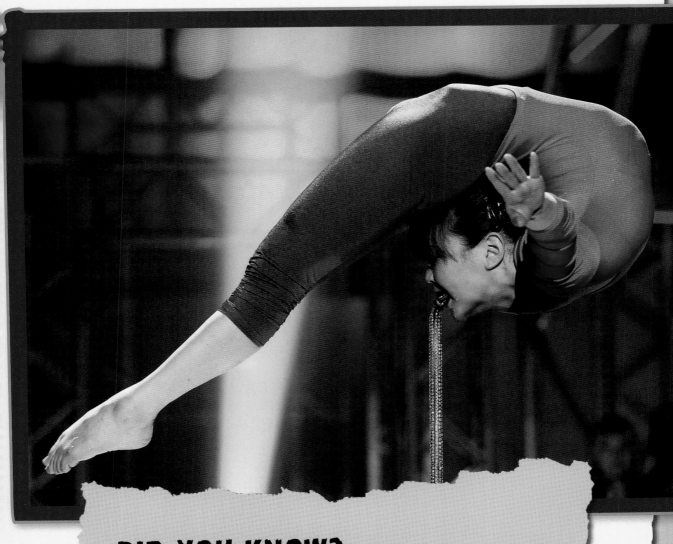

DID YOU KNOW?

In May 2009 a **contortionist** called Iona Luvsandorj did a back bend for 33 seconds. She held herself up just by using her mouth!

Clowning around

Clowns make people laugh by doing funny **skits** or tricks. There are many types of clown. Whiteface clowns wear white makeup and look sad.

Whiteface clown

Auguste (say *aw-GUST*) clowns have a big mouth and eyes and wear bright clothes. Character clowns might wear beards and torn clothes.

Every clown is different. They go
to a special school to learn how to
become clowns. At clown school they
decide what type of clown they will be.
They choose their clown name, clothes,
and makeup, and practise their acts.

character clown

Fun fact: Joeys everywhere

Joseph "Joey" Grimaldi was a clown in England in the early 1800s. He became famous. Clowns today are sometimes called "Joeys" after him.

Animal show

Some circuses have animal acts. Good circuses treat their animals well.

Circus staff feed and clean the animals. **Veterinarians** help if an animal gets ill or is injured. They keep the animals healthy.

Could you work in a circus?

Do you want to be a circus **performer**? They exercise and practise every day. They can't be shy in front of crowds.

Children perform in circuses too.
They still have to do schoolwork.
Circuses travel away from home
for most of the year. The circus staff
becomes the performers' family.

Glossary

aerialist person who performs in the air

cannonball round object shot from a cannon

cirque modern circus that tells a story

contortionist person who can bend their body into extreme positions

daredevil person who performs dangerous tricks

performer person who does something in front of a crowd

ringmaster person who announces the circus acts

skit a short, funny act

somersault tumbling head over feet

trapeze a swing held high in the air

veterinarian animal doctor

Find out more

Books to read

Be A Clown!: Techniques from a Real Clown, Ron Burgess, (Williamson Publishing, 2001)

Cirque Du Soleil, Julie Ferris (Dorling Kindersley, 2008)

Websites

http://www.ringling.com/TopLanding.aspx?id=11610
This website includes circus games, puzzles, and quizzes. It also tells you more about circus history and fun facts.

http://learnhowtojuggle.info
This website shows you how to juggle step-by-step. It includes pictures to follow.

Index